Adult MAD LIBS™

The world's greatest _party_ game

Party Girl Mad Libs

by Roger Price & Leonard Stern

PRICE STERN SLOAN
An Imprint of Penguin Group (USA) Inc.

PRICE STERN SLOAN
Published by the Penguin Group
Penguin Group (USA) Inc., 375 Hudson Street, New York, New York 10014, USA
Penguin Group (Canada), 90 Eglinton Avenue East, Suite 700, Toronto, Ontario M4P 2Y3, Canada
(a division of Pearson Penguin Canada Inc.)
Penguin Books Ltd., 80 Strand, London WC2R 0RL, England
Penguin Group Ireland, 25 St. Stephen's Green, Dublin 2, Ireland
(a division of Penguin Books Ltd.)
Penguin Group (Australia), 250 Camberwell Road, Camberwell, Victoria 3124, Australia
(a division of Pearson Australia Group Pty. Ltd.)
Penguin Books India Pvt. Ltd., 11 Community Centre, Panchsheel Park, New Delhi—110 017, India
Penguin Group (NZ), 67 Apollo Drive, Rosedale, Auckland 0632, New Zealand
(a division of Pearson New Zealand Ltd.)
Penguin Books (South Africa) (Pty.) Ltd., 24 Sturdee Avenue,
Rosebank, Johannesburg 2196, South Africa

Penguin Books Ltd., Registered Offices: 80 Strand, London WC2R 0RL, England

First published in 2006 by Roadside Amusements, a member of Penguin Group (USA) Inc.,
and in 2009 by Price Stern Sloan, an imprint of Penguin Group (USA) Inc.

Cover photograph © iStockphoto/Thinkstock

This edition published in 2012 by Price Stern Sloan,
a division of Penguin Young Readers Group,
345 Hudson Street, New York, New York 10014.

ISBN 978-0-8431-8925-4
3 5 7 9 10 8 6 4

PSS! and *MAD LIBS* are registered trademarks of Penguin Group (USA) Inc.
ADULT MAD LIBS is a trademark of Penguin Group (USA) Inc.

ALWAYS LEARNING   **PEARSON**

MAD LIBS® is a game for people who don't like games!
It can be played by one, two, three, four, or forty.

• RIDICULOUSLY SIMPLE DIRECTIONS

In this tablet you will find stories containing blank spaces where words are left out. One player, the READER, selects one of these stories. The READER does not tell anyone what the story is about. Instead, he/she asks the other players, the WRITERS, to give him/her words. These words are used to fill in the blank spaces in the story.

• TO PLAY

The READER asks each WRITER in turn to call out a word—an adjective or a noun or whatever the space calls for—and uses them to fill in the blank spaces in the story. The result is a MAD LIBS® game.

When the READER then reads the completed MAD LIBS® game to the other players, they will discover that they have written a story that is fantastic, screamingly funny, shocking, silly, crazy, or just plain dumb—depending upon which words each WRITER called out.

• EXAMPLE (*Before* and *After*)

"_____!" he said _____
　　　EXCLAMATION　　　　　　　　　　　ADVERB

as he jumped into his convertible _____ and
　　　　　　　　　　　　　　　　　　　　NOUN

drove off with his _____ wife.
　　　　　　　　　ADJECTIVE

"_____*Ouch*_____!" he said _____*stupidly*_____
　　　EXCLAMATION　　　　　　　　　　　ADVERB

as he jumped into his convertible _____*cat*_____ and
　　　　　　　　　　　　　　　　　　　NOUN

drove off with his _____*brave*_____ wife.
　　　　　　　　　ADJECTIVE

The world's greatest _party_ game

In case you have forgotten what adjectives, adverbs, nouns, and verbs are, here is a quick review:

An **ADJECTIVE** describes something or somebody. *Lumpy, soft, ugly, messy,* and *short* are adjectives.

An **ADVERB** tells how something is done. It modifies a verb and usually ends in "ly." *Modestly, stupidly, greedily,* and *carefully* are adverbs.

A **NOUN** is the name of a person, place, or thing. *Sidewalk, umbrella, bridle, bathtub,* and *nose* are nouns.

A **VERB** is an action word. *Run, pitch, jump,* and *swim* are verbs. Put the verbs in past tense if the directions say **PAST TENSE**. *Ran, pitched, jumped,* and *swam* are verbs in the past tense.

When we ask for **A PLACE**, we mean any sort of place: a country or city (*Spain, Cleveland*) or a room (*bathroom, kitchen*).

An **EXCLAMATION** or **SILLY WORD** is any sort of funny sound, gasp, grunt, or outcry, like *Wow!, Ouch!, Whomp!, Ick!,* and *Gadzooks!*

When we ask for specific words, like a **NUMBER**, a **COLOR**, an **ANIMAL**, or a **PART OF THE BODY**, we mean a word that is one of those things, like *seven, blue, horse,* or *head.*

When we ask for a **PLURAL**, it means more than one. For example, *cat* pluralized is *cats.*

Adult MAD LIBS — HIS HORRORSCOPE

The world's greatest _party_ game

MAD LIBS® is fun to play with friends, but you can also play it by yourself! To begin with, DO NOT look at the story on the page below. Fill in the blanks on this page with the words called for. Then, using the words you have selected, fill in the blank spaces in the story. Now you've created your own hilarious MAD LIBS® game!

PART OF THE BODY _____

ADJECTIVE _____

NOUN _____

VERB ENDING IN "ING" _____

NOUN _____

NOUN _____

ADJECTIVE _____

ADJECTIVE _____

ADJECTIVE _____

NOUN _____

ADJECTIVE _____

PART OF THE BODY _____

NOUN _____

ADJECTIVE _____

NOUN _____

PERSON IN ROOM _____

ADVERB _____

ADVERB _____

ADJECTIVE _____

As you take one last look at your _____ in the mirror, you spy
_{PART OF THE BODY}

a copy of a/an _____ women's magazine on your coffee
_{ADJECTIVE}

_____ . You decide to read your date's horoscope for today.
_{NOUN}

"Beware, Mercury is in retrograde. You will find yourself

_____ at work, but don't fly off the _____ . You could
_{VERB ENDING IN "ING"} _{NOUN}

lose your _____ . You are in the _____ mood to take
_{NOUN} _{ADJECTIVE}

_____ chances in your _____ life, but not until Venus
_{ADJECTIVE} _{ADJECTIVE}

realigns with its _____ . Due to the _____ rash on your
_{NOUN} _{ADJECTIVE}

_____ , your love life is in the _____ for the next three
_{PART OF THE BODY} _{NOUN}

months. A/An _____ person will come into your life and
_{ADJECTIVE}

change your _____ . Resist the urge to call _____ for
_{NOUN} _{PERSON IN ROOM}

help. You're bound to be _____ disappointed and _____
_{ADVERB} _{ADVERB}

depressed." Maybe this date wasn't such a/an _____ idea.
_{ADJECTIVE}

The world's greatest _party_ game

MAD LIBS® is fun to play with friends, but you can also play it by yourself! To begin with, DO NOT look at the story on the page below. Fill in the blanks on this page with the words called for. Then, using the words you have selected, fill in the blank spaces in the story. Now you've created your own hilarious MAD LIBS® game!

NOUN _____

ADJECTIVE _____

ADJECTIVE _____

PLURAL NOUN _____

NOUN _____

ADJECTIVE _____

PLURAL NOUN _____

PART OF THE BODY (PLURAL) _____

PLURAL NOUN _____

PLURAL NOUN _____

NOUN _____

NOUN _____

THE CLOSET

The world's greatest _party_ game

What to wear? If you decide to strap on your favorite low-cut

_____ , he might think it's in _____ taste. Should
NOUN   ADJECTIVE

you decide to slip into your _____ skirt, remember you
                              ADJECTIVE

don't have a blouse and _____ to match. You could wear
                          PLURAL NOUN

your little black halter _____ , but it has a/an
                          NOUN

_____ stain on it. Your tight _____ make you look
ADJECTIVE   PLURAL NOUN

too broad in the _____ . Your silk blouse reveals too much
                  PART OF THE BODY (PLURAL)

of your _____ and your tea-length skirt shows far too little
         PLURAL NOUN

of your _____ . _Sigh_ . . . you finally decide to wear your
         PLURAL NOUN

trusty _____ and hope he doesn't notice you wore it to meet
        NOUN

his mother and _____ .
                NOUN

MAD LIBS® is fun to play with friends, but you can also play it by yourself! To begin with, DO NOT look at the story on the page below. Fill in the blanks on this page with the words called for. Then, using the words you have selected, fill in the blank spaces in the story. Now you've created your own hilarious MAD LIBS® game!

A PLACE _____

CELEBRITY _____

PLURAL NOUN _____

PLURAL NOUN _____

VERB ENDING IN "ING" _____

PLURAL NOUN _____

VERB _____

SAME VERB _____

PART OF THE BODY _____

VERB (PAST TENSE) _____

ADJECTIVE _____

ADJECTIVE _____

NOUN _____

The world's greatest _party_ game

Are you a party girl? Take this quiz and find out!

1. The best part of living in a party town like (the) _____ is:
   <u>A PLACE</u>

   A. increased chances of running into _____.
      <u>CELEBRITY</u>

   B. great transportation! It's easy to get around on public

   _____ and _____.
   <u>PLURAL NOUN</u>   <u>PLURAL NOUN</u>

2. Have you ever stayed up all night _____ with your
   <u>VERB ENDING IN "ING"</u>

   _____ even though you promised yourself you'd get to
   <u>PLURAL NOUN</u>

   _____ early that night?
   <u>VERB</u>

   A. Um, I never _____ before midnight.
      <u>SAME VERB</u>

   B. I fall asleep as soon as my _____ hits the pillow.
      <u>PART OF THE BODY</u>

3. The last time you _____ in on a Saturday night was:
   <u>VERB (PAST TENSE)</u>

   A. in the womb. Want _____ proof? Ask Mom, she'll tell
      <u>ADJECTIVE</u>

   you I've been _____ since birth.
   <u>ADJECTIVE</u>

   B. I stay in every Saturday _____!
      <u>NOUN</u>

If you chose mostly *A*s, you are a party girl. If you chose mostly *B*s,

you need to get out more.

MAD LIBS® is fun to play with friends, but you can also play it by yourself! To begin with, DO NOT look at the story on the page below. Fill in the blanks on this page with the words called for. Then, using the words you have selected, fill in the blank spaces in the story. Now you've created your own hilarious MAD LIBS® game!

TYPE OF LIQUID _____

VERB ENDING IN "ING" _____

VERB ENDING IN "ING" _____

PLURAL NOUN _____

ADJECTIVE _____

ADJECTIVE _____

ANIMAL _____

ADJECTIVE _____

PLURAL NOUN _____

VERB _____

NOUN _____

NOUN _____

PART OF THE BODY _____

NOUN _____

ADJECTIVE _____

NOUN _____

The world's greatest _party_ game

You and your friends all have signature cocktails, even though you'll

drink _____ if you have to. Here are a few drinks and what
TYPE OF LIQUID

each one says about a person.

Beer: You're one of the guys, equally comfortable _____ hot
VERB ENDING IN "ING"

dogs at a ball game or _____ your hand in Texas Hold 'em.
VERB ENDING IN "ING"

Wine: You're a culture vulture who likes to describe both

_____ and wine as _____ and _____.
PLURAL NOUN   ADJECTIVE   ADJECTIVE

Martini: You're a lounge _____ who prowls the
ANIMAL

_____ spots for sophisticated _____ to
ADJECTIVE   PLURAL NOUN

_____.
VERB

Cosmopolitan: You're just a girly _____ who watches too
NOUN

many reruns of _____ _and the City._
NOUN

Margarita: _____-loose and fancy free, you'll strip down to
PART OF THE BODY

your _____ if encouraged.
NOUN

Water: Healthy, _____, and well-hydrated, you're sure to be
ADJECTIVE

popular . . . as the designated _____!
NOUN

Adult MAD LIBS
THE RIGHT PARTY LOOK

The world's greatest _party_ game

MAD LIBS® is fun to play with friends, but you can also play it by yourself! To begin with, DO NOT look at the story on the page below. Fill in the blanks on this page with the words called for. Then, using the words you have selected, fill in the blank spaces in the story. Now you've created your own hilarious MAD LIBS® game!

ADJECTIVE _____

CELEBRITY (FEMALE) _____

ADJECTIVE _____

PART OF THE BODY (PLURAL) _____

NOUN _____

A PLACE _____

COLOR _____

NOUN _____

ADVERB _____

PLURAL NOUN _____

ADJECTIVE _____

ADJECTIVE _____

ADJECTIVE _____

ADJECTIVE _____

PLURAL NOUN _____

NOUN _____

ADJECTIVE _____

THE RIGHT PARTY LOOK

We all have that one feature or accessory that makes us feel

_____ and makes us look like _____ on her most
    ADJECTIVE   CELEBRITY (FEMALE)

_____ day.
    ADJECTIVE

Soft hair: Strangers will want to run their _____ through it
                                                    PART OF THE BODY (PLURAL)

and pet it like their favorite _____ .
                                    NOUN

Smoky eyes: make you look like you come from (the) _____ .
                                                          A PLACE

Full _____ **lips:** Make every _____ in the place
        COLOR   NOUN

want to kiss you _____ .
                          ADVERB

Soft hands: Every man wants to be caressed by the soft

_____ of a/an _____ woman.
   PLURAL NOUN   ADJECTIVE

Short skirt: allows for a/an _____ imagination and very
                                    ADJECTIVE

_____ thoughts.
    ADJECTIVE

Shapely legs: bound to make a/an _____ impression on all
                                    ADJECTIVE

the leg _____ at the party.
        PLURAL NOUN

Stilettos: can be used as a/an _____ during a/an
                                    NOUN

_____ situation.
    ADJECTIVE

Adult MAD LIBS™ — YOUR INTERNET PROFILE

The world's greatest _party_ game

MAD LIBS® is fun to play with friends, but you can also play it by yourself! To begin with, DO NOT look at the story on the page below. Fill in the blanks on this page with the words called for. Then, using the words you have selected, fill in the blank spaces in the story. Now you've created your own hilarious MAD LIBS® game!

ANIMAL _____

PART OF THE BODY _____

ADJECTIVE _____

ADVERB _____

NOUN _____

ADJECTIVE _____

CELEBRITY (MALE) _____

ADJECTIVE _____

NOUN _____

NOUN _____

ADJECTIVE _____

NOUN _____

NOUN _____

PART OF THE BODY (PLURAL) _____

NOUN _____

Why you should get to know me: I'm a cheeky _____ who
ANIMAL

likes to party like a rock star. I have a gorgeous _____ and
PART OF THE BODY

a/an _____ wit.
ADJECTIVE

Who I'm looking for: someone who is _____ sophisticated,
ADVERB

who has traveled around the _____ and speaks many
NOUN

_____ languages. It won't hurt if he looks like
ADJECTIVE

_____ . But appearances aren't everything. He should also
CELEBRITY (MALE)

have a very _____ bank account.
ADJECTIVE

Three things I can't live without: a good _____ to read, my
NOUN

cell _____ , and my _____ curiosity.
NOUN   ADJECTIVE

Best (or worst) lie I've ever told: "I left my _____ in my
NOUN

other _____ , Officer!"
NOUN

Place I wish I were right now: in the _____ of a loving
PART OF THE BODY (PLURAL)

_____ .
NOUN

MAD LIBS® is fun to play with friends, but you can also play it by yourself! To begin with, DO NOT look at the story on the page below. Fill in the blanks on this page with the words called for. Then, using the words you have selected, fill in the blank spaces in the story. Now you've created your own hilarious MAD LIBS® game!

CITY _____

NOUN _____

CELEBRITY (MALE) _____

SAME CITY _____

SAME CELEBRITY (MALE) _____

NUMBER _____

VERB _____

NOUN _____

ADJECTIVE _____

NOUN _____

PLURAL NOUN _____

PLURAL NOUN _____

PART OF THE BODY (PLURAL) _____

OCCUPATION _____

PART OF THE BODY _____

NOUN _____

VERB _____

NUMBER _____

NUMBER _____

_____ Hilton just called with an invitation to a
CITY

party that's being thrown at Chez _____, the new
NOUN

restaurant owned by _____. _____ says
CELEBRITY (MALE)   SAME CITY

_____ has been asking for you and hopes you will be there
SAME CELEBRITY (MALE)

tonight. She says she'll pick you up in _____ minutes. You
NUMBER

_____ to your _____, throw on your
VERB   NOUN

_____ _____, and run out the door just as the
ADJECTIVE   NOUN

limo is pulling up. You jump in and someone hands you a bottle of

_____. As you pull up to the restaurant, you see the
PLURAL NOUN

paparazzi. They put their _____ up to their _____
PLURAL NOUN   PART OF THE BODY (PLURAL)

and wait. The _____ opens the door, and you're the first one
OCCUPATION

out. As you place one _____ on the red _____, the
PART OF THE BODY   NOUN

cameras start flashing. You can't _____. You lose your step
VERB

and fall facedown in front of _____ people. You didn't make
NUMBER

it into the party, but you did make _Page_ _____.
NUMBER

The world's greatest _party_ game

MAD LIBS® is fun to play with friends, but you can also play it by yourself! To begin with, DO NOT look at the story on the page below. Fill in the blanks on this page with the words called for. Then, using the words you have selected, fill in the blank spaces in the story. Now you've created your own hilarious MAD LIBS® game!

VERB _____

ADJECTIVE _____

NOUN _____

PART OF THE BODY _____

NOUN _____

PART OF THE BODY _____

ADJECTIVE _____

ADJECTIVE _____

ADJECTIVE _____

NOUN _____

NOUN _____

PART OF THE BODY (PLURAL) _____

The world's greatest _party_ game

Flirting takes skill. It's not something you can _____
VERB

overnight. However, here are a few tips to put you on your way to

becoming a/an _____ flirt.
ADJECTIVE

- When you spy a/an _____ to whom you are attracted,
NOUN

  make _____ contact immediately. If possible, find a
  PART OF THE BODY

  mutual _____ who can introduce the two of you.
  NOUN

- Lightly touch his _____ while talking to him.
  PART OF THE BODY

- Tell him you think he's a/an _____ conversationalist.
  ADJECTIVE

- Laugh out loud at his _____ jokes even if they aren't
  ADJECTIVE

  _____ .
  ADJECTIVE

- Compliment him on the way he wears his _____ or
  NOUN

  his beautiful speaking _____ .
  NOUN

- Be seductive without being obvious. Always swing your

  _____ when you walk.
  PART OF THE BODY (PLURAL)

Adult MAD LIBS™ SPEED DATING

The world's greatest _party_ game

MAD LIBS® is fun to play with friends, but you can also play it by yourself! To begin with, DO NOT look at the story on the page below. Fill in the blanks on this page with the words called for. Then, using the words you have selected, fill in the blank spaces in the story. Now you've created your own hilarious MAD LIBS® game!

ADJECTIVE _____

ADJECTIVE _____

NUMBER _____

NOUN _____

NOUN _____

ANIMAL _____

PART OF THE BODY _____

NOUN _____

ADJECTIVE _____

CELEBRITY (FEMALE) _____

PERSON IN ROOM (MALE) _____

NUMBER _____

NOUN _____

VERB (PAST TENSE) _____

PART OF THE BODY (PLURAL) _____

NOUN _____

PERSON IN ROOM _____

ADJECTIVE _____

SPEED DATING

The world's greatest _party_ game

You can't believe it's come to this: _____ dating. You're
                                          ADJECTIVE

sitting in this _____ restaurant and every _____
                    ADJECTIVE   NUMBER

minutes, you move to another table to meet another _____ .
                                                        NOUN

You've already met a whole bunch of jerks, and you have a/an

_____ in your stomach. The first one spoke as fast as
    NOUN

a/an _____ runs. The second wouldn't look you in
        ANIMAL

the _____ and kept scratching his _____ .
      PART OF THE BODY   NOUN

Next! The third guy was drop-dead _____ . The
                                        ADJECTIVE

problem? He looked like _____ . Now you're sitting
                            CELEBRITY (FEMALE)

across from a guy named _____ who's wearing a
                            PERSON IN ROOM (MALE)

jacket with _____ sleeves and a/an _____ on his
                NUMBER   NOUN

head. "Haven't we _____ somewhere before?"
                      VERB (PAST TENSE)

You roll your _____ and check your _____ . It's
                PART OF THE BODY (PLURAL)   NOUN

seven. Time to get out of here, call _____ , and go grab a/an
                                        PERSON IN ROOM

_____ meal.
    ADJECTIVE

MAD LIBS® is fun to play with friends, but you can also play it by yourself! To begin with, DO NOT look at the story on the page below. Fill in the blanks on this page with the words called for. Then, using the words you have selected, fill in the blank spaces in the story. Now you've created your own hilarious MAD LIBS® game!

PART OF THE BODY _____

ADJECTIVE _____

VERB _____

CELEBRITY (MALE) _____

PLURAL NOUN _____

ADJECTIVE _____

NOUN _____

NOUN _____

ANIMAL _____

NOUN _____

ADVERB _____

NOUN _____

NOUN _____

NOUN _____

Adult MAD LIBS™ GOOD GIRL... OR BAD?

The world's greatest _party_ game

It can feel so good to be bad. Do you tend to be more angel or vixen?

Take this little quiz and be honest (at least with yourself).

Would you:

1. wear a dress with a plunging _____-line to look
PART OF THE BODY

   _____?
   ADJECTIVE

2. _____ with _____ on a first date?
VERB   CELEBRITY (MALE)

3. take office _____ from work?
PLURAL NOUN

4. spread _____ rumors about your friends?
ADJECTIVE

5. return the leather _____ you found in the ladies'
NOUN

   _____ at the club?
   NOUN

6. drink like a/an _____?
ANIMAL

7. light up a/an _____ even though you know it's
NOUN

   _____ dangerous?
   ADVERB

8. bump into a parked _____ and leave the scene of the
NOUN

   _____?
   NOUN

If you answered mostly yes, you are definitely a bad _____.
NOUN

Adult MAD LIBS™ — A GIRL AND HER FRIENDS

The world's greatest _party_ game

MAD LIBS® is fun to play with friends, but you can also play it by yourself! To begin with, DO NOT look at the story on the page below. Fill in the blanks on this page with the words called for. Then, using the words you have selected, fill in the blank spaces in the story. Now you've created your own hilarious MAD LIBS® game!

ADJECTIVE _____

ADJECTIVE _____

ADVERB _____

VERB _____

PLURAL NOUN _____

NOUN _____

ADJECTIVE _____

ADJECTIVE _____

PLURAL NOUN _____

PART OF THE BODY _____

NOUN _____

NOUN _____

ADJECTIVE _____

SILLY WORD _____

NOUN _____

NOUN _____

A GIRL AND HER FRIENDS

Every girl needs a few _____ girlfriends to hit the town
                         ADJECTIVE

with. Friends who will stick by you through thick or _____.
                                                        ADJECTIVE

Friends who will _____ share the check and not quibble
                    ADVERB

over whose turn it is to _____ the next round.
                            VERB

_____ you can call at the very last minute to be ready when
PLURAL NOUN

you roll up in your convertible _____ with a/an
                                    NOUN

_____ invitation to a/an _____ party. Friends
ADJECTIVE   ADJECTIVE

you've known for many _____, who have nursed you
                          PLURAL NOUN

through a broken _____, cheered when you got that well-
                    PART OF THE BODY

deserved _____, and agreed that your designer
            NOUN

_____ was a/an _____ steal. Most importantly,
NOUN   ADJECTIVE

these friends know the type of guy you go _____ over and
                                              SILLY WORD

won't think twice about approaching someone who fits the

description of your dream _____ and asking, "What do you
                            NOUN

think of my beautiful _____ over there?" Ahh, true
                          NOUN

friendship . . .

Adult MAD LIBS — DISCO FEVER

The world's greatest _party_ game

MAD LIBS® is fun to play with friends, but you can also play it by yourself! To begin with, DO NOT look at the story on the page below. Fill in the blanks on this page with the words called for. Then, using the words you have selected, fill in the blank spaces in the story. Now you've created your own hilarious MAD LIBS® game!

CELEBRITY (FEMALE) _____

PART OF THE BODY _____

NOUN _____

VERB ENDING IN "ING" _____

NOUN _____

ADJECTIVE _____

NOUN _____

VERB ENDING IN "ING" _____

VERB ENDING IN "ING" _____

ADVERB _____

ADVERB _____

PLURAL NOUN _____

PLURAL NOUN _____

PART OF THE BODY (PLURAL) _____

NOUN _____

NUMBER _____

ADJECTIVE _____

NOUN _____

Adult MAD LIBS™ — DISCO FEVER

The world's greatest _party_ game

You like to dance. Everyone knows it. It started when you saw

_____ shaking her _____ at a/an _____
CELEBRITY (FEMALE)   PART OF THE BODY   NOUN

event. You were hooked and you decided to take _____
VERB ENDING IN "ING"

classes! They cost you an arm and a/an _____, and every
NOUN

weekend you head to a/an _____ nightclub and blow a
ADJECTIVE

small _____ on cover charges to practice your
NOUN

_____. At first you are shy. You start by _____ at
VERB ENDING IN "ING"   VERB ENDING IN "ING"

the edge of the dance floor and _____ work your way to the
ADVERB

center. You _____ realize you're no longer shy, and you're
ADVERB

making all the right _____. A crowd gathers, shouting
PLURAL NOUN

_____ of encouragement at the top of their _____.
PLURAL NOUN   PART OF THE BODY (PLURAL)

You love it. You dance your _____ out. You take
NOUN

_____ bows to _____ applause. And you can truly
NUMBER   ADJECTIVE

say you're a real _____!
NOUN

Adult MAD LIBS™ SPRING BREAK

The world's greatest _party_ game

MAD LIBS® is fun to play with friends, but you can also play it by yourself! To begin with, DO NOT look at the story on the page below. Fill in the blanks on this page with the words called for. Then, using the words you have selected, fill in the blank spaces in the story. Now you've created your own hilarious MAD LIBS® game!

ADJECTIVE _____

A PLACE _____

PLURAL NOUN _____

ADJECTIVE _____

NUMBER _____

PERSON IN ROOM _____

EXCLAMATION _____

NOUN _____

NOUN _____

NOUN _____

OCCUPATION _____

NOUN _____

NOUN _____

For months, you and your friends have been saving for the ultimate

spring break vacation. After many _____ discussions, you've
ADJECTIVE

all decided that (the) _____ is the perfect place to party. You
A PLACE

spent weeks dreaming about all the hot _____ you would
PLURAL NOUN

meet, the _____ daiquiris you would consume, and how you
ADJECTIVE

wouldn't sleep for _____ days. You booked the hotel and
NUMBER

were thrilled to find such a great rate. But once you arrived,

_____ took one look and exclaimed, " _____ ! This
PERSON IN ROOM   EXCLAMATION

place is a/an _____ ." You decide to go down to the
NOUN

_____ for a quick swim. But as soon as you open the door,
NOUN

the _____ rings. It's the desk _____ telling you that
NOUN   OCCUPATION

a hundred mile per hour _____ is heading in the hotel's
NOUN

direction and that you'll have to pack your _____ and get
NOUN

out as soon as possible. So much for spring break.

A DANGEROUS COCKTAIL

The world's greatest *party* game

MAD LIBS® is fun to play with friends, but you can also play it by yourself! To begin with, DO NOT look at the story on the page below. Fill in the blanks on this page with the words called for. Then, using the words you have selected, fill in the blank spaces in the story. Now you've created your own hilarious MAD LIBS® game!

ADJECTIVE _badass_

PERSON IN ROOM _Alicia_

NOUN _tennis ball_

NOUN _sexpot_

PLURAL NOUN _twinks_

NOUN _flag_

NOUN _recipe_

NOUN _hero_

ADVERB _chillingly_

NOUN _ghost_

NOUN _soul_

ADJECTIVE _horny_

COLOR _red_

NOUN _follicles_

PERSON IN ROOM _Alicia_

ADJECTIVE _bangin_

NOUN _body_

Adult MAD LIBS™ A DANGEROUS COCKTAIL

The world's greatest _party_ game

It's your first time playing bartender and you're feeling a little

_____. As a test, before _____ arrives, you
    ADJECTIVE   PERSON IN ROOM

decide to mix a/an _____ for yourself. Maybe it will become
                NOUN

a smash at the _____ event. Maybe you'll go down in the
           NOUN

history _____ as a beverage visionary. It would definitely
    PLURAL NOUN

beat your day job in _____ sales. You pick up the
             NOUN

_____ juice and pour a generous amount into a/an
  NOUN

_____ and shake it _____. Then you add a sprig
  NOUN   ADVERB

of _____ and a dash of _____. Unexpectedly, it
   NOUN   NOUN

starts to bubble and turns a/an _____ shade of
               ADJECTIVE

_____. You let out a screeching _____ and quickly
  COLOR   NOUN

decide that _____ will tend bar tonight. So ends your short,
    PERSON IN ROOM

_____ career as a/an _____-tender extraordinaire!
  ADJECTIVE   NOUN

OFFICE PARTY OATH

The world's greatest _party_ game

MAD LIBS® is fun to play with friends, but you can also play it by yourself! To begin with, DO NOT look at the story on the page below. Fill in the blanks on this page with the words called for. Then, using the words you have selected, fill in the blank spaces in the story. Now you've created your own hilarious MAD LIBS® game!

ADJECTIVE _____

ADJECTIVE _____

NOUN _____

PART OF THE BODY _____

NOUN _____

NOUN _____

ADJECTIVE _____

PART OF THE BODY _____

NOUN _____

TYPE OF FOOD _____

NOUN _____

NOUN _____

ADJECTIVE _____

PERSON IN ROOM _____

OFFICE PARTY OATH

Tonight is the _____ office holiday party, and I do hereby
ADJECTIVE

promise that I will not make the same _____ mistakes as
ADJECTIVE

last year. I will not drink too much _____-nog
NOUN

and fall on my _____. When my boss wishes me
PART OF THE BODY

a merry _____, I will not shout, "What am I? A/An
NOUN

_____-magnet?" I will not sniff near my boss's wife and ask
NOUN

her why she's marinating in such a/an _____ perfume.
ADJECTIVE

I will not make photocopies of my _____ or dance on
PART OF THE BODY

the conference room _____. I will not step in
NOUN

the _____ while dancing on the _____. I
TYPE OF FOOD   NOUN

understand that it does not amuse my colleagues when I joke, "This

isn't an office, it's a/an _____ with fluorescent lighting!"
NOUN

This year I promise I will be on my most _____ behavior,
ADJECTIVE

because, for the love of _____, I can't keep looking for a
PERSON IN ROOM

new job every New Year's Day . . .

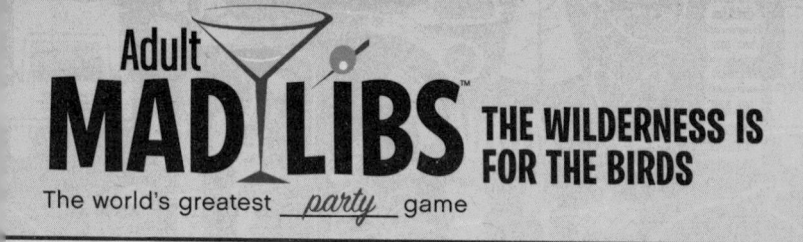

Adult MAD LIBS™

THE WILDERNESS IS FOR THE BIRDS

The world's greatest _party_ game

MAD LIBS® is fun to play with friends, but you can also play it by yourself! To begin with, DO NOT look at the story on the page below. Fill in the blanks on this page with the words called for. Then, using the words you have selected, fill in the blank spaces in the story. Now you've created your own hilarious MAD LIBS® game!

ADJECTIVE _____

NOUN _____

NOUN _____

NOUN _____

COLOR _____

NOUN _____

EXCLAMATION _____

ADJECTIVE _____

NOUN _____

PART OF THE BODY _____

NOUN _____

NOUN _____

PLURAL NOUN _____

NOUN _____

VERB _____

NOUN _____

Adult MAD LIBS™ THE WILDERNESS IS FOR THE BIRDS

The world's greatest __party__ game

Your current boyfriend is passionate about the _____
ADJECTIVE

outdoors. Today, he's taking you hiking. You are wearing

_____ shoes and a comfortable _____. You're at
NOUN   NOUN

the base of a mountain that looks as high as the Empire

_____ Building. You keep up for the first few minutes, but
NOUN

then you start puffing and your face turns _____. Then you
COLOR

spy a wild _____ lurking in the bushes. " _____ !"
NOUN   EXCLAMATION

you yelp as you rub against some _____ ivy and quickly get
ADJECTIVE

a nasty _____ on your leg. Your boyfriend starts to kiss your
NOUN

_____, giving you the courage to go on. Finally, it's
PART OF THE BODY

lunchtime and your date opens his _____. He pulls out
NOUN

a/an _____ and a thermos full of liquid _____. He
NOUN   PLURAL NOUN

expects you to put that in your _____? Is he crazy? You have
NOUN

no choice but to _____, but you say to yourself, "This is the
VERB

last time I commune with Mother _____."
NOUN

From ADULT MAD LIBS™: Party Girl Mad Libs • Copyright © 2009 by Price Stern Sloan, an imprint of Penguin Group (USA) Inc., 345 Hudson Street, New York, NY 10014.

THE WISH LIST

The world's greatest *party* game

MAD LIBS® is fun to play with friends, but you can also play it by yourself! To begin with, DO NOT look at the story on the page below. Fill in the blanks on this page with the words called for. Then, using the words you have selected, fill in the blank spaces in the story. Now you've created your own hilarious MAD LIBS® game!

ADJECTIVE _____

NOUN _____

NOUN _____

NOUN _____

NOUN _____

OCCUPATION _____

NOUN _____

PLURAL NOUN _____

A PLACE _____

NOUN _____

PART OF THE BODY _____

NOUN _____

VERB ENDING IN "ING" _____

TYPE OF LIQUID _____

ADJECTIVE _____

Whether we write it down or not, we all have a/an _____
_{ADJECTIVE}

list of what we're looking for in the perfect mate. For example:

- loves his mother more than his new _____
  _{NOUN}

- can make the rent every month on his _____
  _{NOUN}

- isn't allergic to your pet _____
  _{NOUN}

- can speak _____ fluently
  _{NOUN}

- moonlights as a/an _____
  _{OCCUPATION}

- takes you to _____ games and explains the
  _{NOUN}

  _____ to you
  _{PLURAL NOUN}

- watches old movies like *The Wizard of (the)* _____ and
  _{A PLACE}

  Gone with the _____
  _{NOUN}

- adores your _____
  _{PART OF THE BODY}

- is careful about his health, sprinkling _____ leaves in his
  _{NOUN}

  food and _____ daily to keep fit
  _{VERB ENDING IN "ING"}

- is careful about his appearance, slicking _____ in
  _{TYPE OF LIQUID}

  his hair and _____ lotion on his skin
  _{ADJECTIVE}

THE SCAVENGER HUNT

The world's greatest _party_ game

MAD LIBS® is fun to play with friends, but you can also play it by yourself! To begin with, DO NOT look at the story on the page below. Fill in the blanks on this page with the words called for. Then, using the words you have selected, fill in the blank spaces in the story. Now you've created your own hilarious MAD LIBS® game!

ADJECTIVE _____

NOUN _____

PLURAL NOUN _____

NUMBER _____

PLURAL NOUN _____

PERSON IN ROOM _____

NOUN _____

OCCUPATION _____

NOUN _____

NOUN _____

ADJECTIVE _____

NOUN _____

ADJECTIVE _____

NOUN _____

NOUN _____

NOUN _____

PLURAL NOUN _____

THE SCAVENGER HUNT

The world's greatest _party_ game

Your friends are feeling _____, so you've decided to have a
                        ADJECTIVE

scavenger hunt rather than go to the usual _____ for Friday
                                              NOUN

night _____. You've drawn up a list of things to gather and
       PLURAL NOUN

plan on giving _____ _____ to the victor.
                  NUMBER   PLURAL NOUN

_____ is the first to return, and she/he has found
PERSON IN ROOM

everything, including:

- a digital photo of a/an _____
                            NOUN

- a business card from a/an _____
                              OCCUPATION

- a phone number written on a/an _____
                                    NOUN

- a/an _____ from a/an _____ restaurant
          NOUN   ADJECTIVE

- a/an _____ from a/an _____ strip club
          NOUN   ADJECTIVE

- a live _____ from the nearest zoo
            NOUN

- a ticket stub from a/an _____ concert
                            NOUN

- a toy _____
           NOUN

- a box of used _____
                   PLURAL NOUN

Adult MAD LIBS™ NEW YEAR'S EVE

The world's greatest _party_ game

MAD LIBS® is fun to play with friends, but you can also play it by yourself! To begin with, DO NOT look at the story on the page below. Fill in the blanks on this page with the words called for. Then, using the words you have selected, fill in the blank spaces in the story. Now you've created your own hilarious MAD LIBS® game!

ADJECTIVE _____

NOUN _____

NOUN _____

ADJECTIVE _____

CELEBRITY (FEMALE) _____

ADJECTIVE _____

NUMBER _____

ADJECTIVE _____

NOUN _____

NUMBER _____

PERSON IN ROOM _____

A PLACE _____

NOUN _____

NOUN _____

ADJECTIVE _____

So many choices, but only one night! After the _____
ADJECTIVE

holiday you just spent with your _____ you're ready to let
NOUN

off a little _____. The invites you've received so far are:
NOUN

• a/an _____ party at the home of a/an _____
ADJECTIVE   CELEBRITY (FEMALE)

look-alike

• a/an _____ invitation to go out with your ex whom you
ADJECTIVE

haven't seen in _____ years but still have feelings for
NUMBER

occasionally

• a/an _____ cousin and her _____ think they
ADJECTIVE   NOUN

have the perfect intimate party: a home-cooked dinner for

_____ of their closest friends
NUMBER

But you're thinking that maybe you'll surprise _____, who's
PERSON IN ROOM

visiting (the) _____, and hop a jet _____ in time to
A PLACE   NOUN

have a quick _____ and ring in the _____ New Year!
NOUN   ADJECTIVE

THE BLIND DATE

MAD LIBS® is fun to play with friends, but you can also play it by yourself! To begin with, DO NOT look at the story on the page below. Fill in the blanks on this page with the words called for. Then, using the words you have selected, fill in the blank spaces in the story. Now you've created your own hilarious MAD LIBS® game!

PERSON IN ROOM _____

PERSON IN ROOM (MALE) _____

ADJECTIVE _____

ADJECTIVE _____

NOUN _____

OCCUPATION _____

OCCUPATION _____

CELEBRITY (FEMALE) _____

NOUN _____

VERB (PAST TENSE) _____

NOUN _____

NOUN _____

NOUN _____

NOUN _____

VERB _____

NUMBER _____

ADJECTIVE _____

COLOR _____

PART OF THE BODY _____

VERB _____

Adult MAD LIBS™ — THE BLIND DATE

The world's greatest *party* game

_____ has fixed you up with _____. It's your very
PERSON IN ROOM · PERSON IN ROOM (MALE)

first blind date and, frankly, you're feeling _____.
ADJECTIVE

You haven't seen a picture of him, but he's been described as

_____ and is on a/an _____ team. After a
ADJECTIVE · NOUN

stint as a/an _____, he settled into his current job as
OCCUPATION

a/an _____. He's worked with _____ on a charity
OCCUPATION · CELEBRITY (FEMALE)

_____ ball and apparently _____ with her at her
NOUN · VERB (PAST TENSE)

country _____. You're hoping it works out so you can hang
NOUN

with her at the next _____. He shows up at your
NOUN

_____ with a large _____ in hand. Unfortunately,
NOUN · NOUN

it's not big enough to _____ him. He weighs _____
VERB · NUMBER

pounds, has a/an _____ tooth, and a/an _____
ADJECTIVE · COLOR

blemish on the end of his _____. Oh well, you can always
PART OF THE BODY

close your eyes when you _____ him later. Maybe that's why
VERB

they are called *blind* dates.

MAD LIBS® is fun to play with friends, but you can also play it by yourself! To begin with, DO NOT look at the story on the page below. Fill in the blanks on this page with the words called for. Then, using the words you have selected, fill in the blank spaces in the story. Now you've created your own hilarious MAD LIBS® game!

ADVERB _____

PLURAL NOUN _____

PLURAL NOUN _____

NOUN _____

NOUN _____

VERB _____

ADJECTIVE _____

VERB _____

NUMBER _____

CELEBRITY (MALE) _____

ANIMAL _____

NOUN _____

CELEBRITY (FEMALE) _____

CELEBRITY (FEMALE) _____

NOUN _____

NUMBER _____

PLURAL NOUN _____

PLURAL NOUN _____

Adult MAD LIBS™ SOCIAL COORDINATOR

The world's greatest _party_ game

Is it your fault you're so _____ popular? Of course all your
_{ADVERB}

_____ look to you to fill their _____ with
PLURAL NOUN   PLURAL NOUN

_____ and adventure. Problem is, you're running out of
NOUN

ideas! Your title of "Miss _____ USA" is being threatened,
NOUN

and you've got to _____ fast. But what more could you do?
VERB

You've already scored VIP tickets to that _____ concert
ADJECTIVE

featuring the _____ _____ band. You convinced
VERB   NUMBER

_____ to sneak you into the _____ Club for a
CELEBRITY (MALE)   ANIMAL

private party. You were invited to the _____ party that
NOUN

_____ threw with _____ . Both _____
CELEBRITY (FEMALE)   CELEBRITY (FEMALE)   NOUN

magazine and _Page_ _____ have cited you as the new It Girl,
NUMBER

and even Joan _____ says you have excellent style. Maybe
PLURAL NOUN

you should take a night off and let your _____ fend for
PLURAL NOUN

themselves . . .